PUFFER'S SURPRISE

SMITHSONIAN OCEANIC COLLECTION

To Hannah and A.J. — B.G.W.

For James Daniel and Joseph John — S.J.P

Book layout: Marcin D. Pilchowski
Editor: Laura Gates Galvin
Editorial assistance: Chelsea Shriver

First Edition 2003
10 9 8 7 6 5 4 3 2 1
Printed in Singapore

Acknowledgments:
     Our very special thanks to Dr. Victor Springer of the Department of Systematic Biology at the Smithsonian Institution's National Museum of Natural History for his curatorial review.
     Soundprints would also like to thank Ellen Nanney and Robyn Bissette at the Smithsonian Institution's Office of Product Development and Licensing for their help in the creation of this book.
     The artist would like to acknowledge the curators at the Smithsonian Institution and The New York City Aquarium for their research assistance, Chelsea Shriver at Soundprints for keeping it all together and his family for their constant support.

Library of Congress Cataloging-in-Publication Data
is on file with the publisher and the Library of Congress.

PUFFER'S SURPRISE

by Barbara Gaines Winkelman   Illustrated by Steven James Petruccio

Soundprints
Where Children Discover...

Under the clear blue sea that surrounds the Galapagos Islands, lays a busy coral reef. It is daybreak—a time of change in the reef. Nocturnal fish search out coral nooks where they will sleep, while the fish that are active during the day awaken. A puffer fish begins to stir in his sandy bed.

Dawn is a dangerous time in the deep sea. Sharks and barracudas watch their prey closely, hoping to catch them in a sleepy moment. But Puffer is safe from harm for now. The bull's-eye pattern on his back camouflages him against the sand, making it hard to see him from above.

Once Puffer is awake, he swims out of the sand to eat spiny sea urchins on the ocean floor. He crushes and grinds the urchins with his four sharp teeth. Puffer's teeth never stop growing. Chomping on crunchy foods files them down so they don't grow too long.

A shadow quickly passes over Puffer. It is a school of barracuda. Puffer waits motionless for a moment, then continues to eat, watching the predators closely. Suddenly, one breaks from the school and darts at Puffer!

Quickly, Puffer gulps down water that fills a sac in his stomach. His tough skin stretches out and he becomes twice his original size. Puffer has changed from a quick and easy meal to a balloon that is too big for the barracuda to swallow! The barracuda swims away.

Puffer expels the water he swallowed and returns to his smaller size. Still hungry, Puffer crunches into a snail, then looks for more food. He eats until his stomach is round and bumpy from all the good things stuffed inside.

Puffer swims slowly toward a coral island in the distance. A yellow-orange gleam catches his eye. He swims toward the bright colors and sees a group of rainbow wrasses surrounding an angelfish. Puffer swims closer. The wrasses are cleaning the angelfish. Puffer lines up with other fish that are waiting to be cleaned. He has found one of the cleaning stations that are scattered around the coral reef.

When Puffer reaches the front of the line, the rainbow wrasses nip the dead skin and parasites off him. There is a partnership between the wrasses and the fish being cleaned, like Puffer. Each partner benefits—the wrasses are fed and Puffer stays clean and healthy.

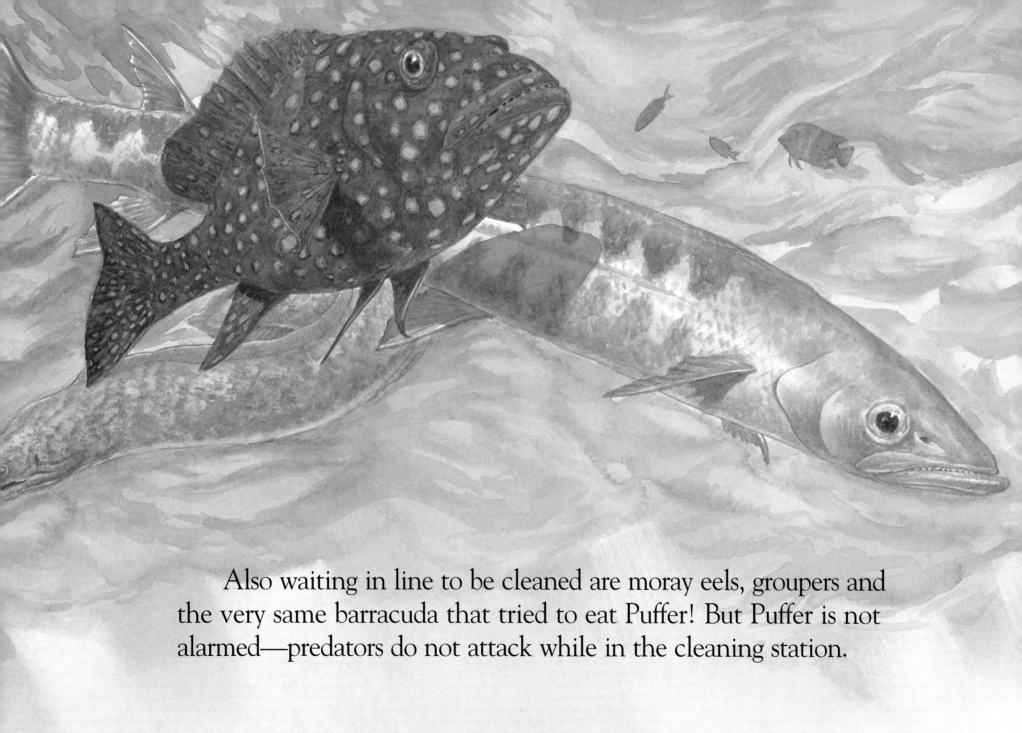

Also waiting in line to be cleaned are moray eels, groupers and the very same barracuda that tried to eat Puffer! But Puffer is not alarmed—predators do not attack while in the cleaning station.

Freshly groomed, Puffer continues to search for a meal. He stops suddenly, sensing danger. He turns around. Swimming right toward him is a large spotted sea bass!

Puffer blows up like a beach ball as the sea bass attacks. The sea bass catches Puffer in his throat, but Puffer is too big for the sea bass to swallow! The sea bass has no choice but to spit Puffer out into the water. As the sea bass turns around, Puffer slowly swims away.

But the sea bass hasn't given up and once again he lunges toward Puffer. Puffer darts into a hole in the reef and swells up. He is too big to be pulled out by the sea bass. This time the sea bass leaves to look for other prey. He is gone for good.

Puffer continues searching for food. A banded blenny swims too close to Puffer. Puffer nips at his fins and the blenny swims away. Puffer hunts and feeds alone.

It is dusk at the reef. Now the nocturnal fish awaken to look for food, while the fish that have been swimming and eating all day look for places to hide in the coral. With his bull's-eye pattern keeping him hidden under the moonlight, Puffer settles in the sand for a peaceful night.

About the Puffer Fish

One of the most unusual looking fish in the ocean, the puffer fish lives in all tropical and temperate seas. Most species prefer to stay near the bottom of the ocean where they blend in with coral reefs. A few species swim in the open ocean. Some puffer fish live in brackish and fresh water.

There are over 100 species of puffer fish, also known as blowfish, swellfish, globefish and rabbitfish. Some species of puffer fish are covered with spines, but many are not.

Puffer fish are carnivores and eat crustaceans, sea urchins, sponges and mollusks. They crush and grind their prey with their sharp, fused teeth.

When puffer fish become threatened, they gulp air or water, filling a special sac found inside their bodies. This gives puffer fish a balloon-like appearance. Their skin is thick and somewhat leathery, and they have no ribs or pelvic bones.

Puffer fish are generally small at approximately 3 to 20 inches long. However, there are some puffers that reach more than three feet, which makes their swollen state quite a sight to see!

Glossary

coral reef: A hard substance under tropical waters that is made up of the skeletons of small sea animals.

nocturnal: Animals and fish that are active at night and sleep during the day.

camouflage: The ability to hide and blend into a background.

predator: An animal that kills another animal for food.

expel: To drive or force out.

parasite: An organism that lives on another organism.

Points of Interest in This Book

pp. 4-5: black-striped salema (right).

pp. 6-7: scalloped hammerhead shark (center); white tip reef shark (right).

pp. 8-9: sea urchin (lower left).

pp. 12-13: barracuda.

pp. 14-15: blue-and-gold snapper (left); parrot fish (center); sea snail.

pp. 18-19: fan worm (upper left); rainbow wrasses; anemone (lower left).

pp. 24-25: spotted sea bass.

pp. 28-29: shrimp (lower left); trumpet fish (below Puffer); banded blenny (lower right).

pp. 30-31: squirrel fish (yellow mottled fish); cardinal fish (orange fish).